50 POETIC TALES OF COMPONENTS AND QUANTITIES

A POETRY BOOK

KSHITISH SHARMA

Copyright © Kshitish Sharma
All Rights Reserved.

ISBN 979-888521344-8

This book has been published with all efforts taken to make the material error-free after the consent of the author. However, the author and the publisher do not assume and hereby disclaim any liability to any party for any loss, damage, or disruption caused by errors or omissions, whether such errors or omissions result from negligence, accident, or any other cause.

While every effort has been made to avoid any mistake or omission, this publication is being sold on the condition and understanding that neither the author nor the publishers or printers would be liable in any manner to any person by reason of any mistake or omission in this publication or for any action taken or omitted to be taken or advice rendered or accepted on the basis of this work. For any defect in printing or binding the publishers will be liable only to replace the defective copy by another copy of this work then available.

Contents

Contents

Contents

1. Stress and strain chat

Strain told to stress I am in a pain,
You have compressed me again and again.
Either tensile, compressive or in a shear,
Can't you do me a favour to spare?
Stress said where I will act I will push you,
Either it is shear or tensile it is up to you.
You are an important thing to calculate,
Poisson ratio is your good mate.
Just enjoy with me your typical curve,
Ductile, brittle or a fracture point curve.
Our life is hectic and very fantastic,
Either for a elastic, brittle or a plastic.

2. Shear force and bending moment tale

Shear force and bending moment is a team,
Acting at the end or all along the beam.
Tangled with a point loads,uniform or varying,
Cantilevered at the end with a moment of bending.
Bending moment is a tricky one,
Sometimes rectangular,triangular or a parabolic one.
Simple supported with a single hinge,
Rollers support giving a lot to think.
Then comes the point of lecture,
Just calculate the point of contraflexure.
Taking the section from left to right,
Both these diagrams are in the limelight.

3. Twist and torsion

So many turns and so many twists,
Equation of torsion is in the list.
With assuming of just a shaft,
Hollow or Solid with a long task.
Comes the polar moment and torque ,
With an idea to calculate the power.
Moment of inertia just baffles the mind,
Power units from kilowatt to watt not so kind.
At last comes the shafts on parallel and series,
Giving a sigh of relief in the twists.

4. Ductile and brittle banter

Ductile once taunted a brittle,
You just fail quickly with a pull of little.
I am more famous than you and more furious,
All my chips are smooth and continuous.
Brittle said I am not little,
Sometimes I too have a giggle.
Many materials like Cast Iron are my trademark,
I am the one which is used for many tasks.
If I am brittle I am also hard,
That is what is difficult for you to talk.
We both are running the material science,
Cast iron or you as a mild steel or in the bench vice.
We should not fight much ,
We both love each other so much.

5. A column with different shades

Column coming with an axial load,
Has to bear a lot of heavy workload.
Becomes a tedious task to calculate,
From short to long all are just a headache.
Euler theory will come to work,
Crippling load will become our work.
When hinged it is the same,
When fixed it is a half game.
When fixed and free it is a double,
When fixed and hinged it is just seventy percent.
Cases which are hard to bear,
Slenderness ratio has to help and care.

6. Deflection with slope

Gone are the shear force and bending moment,
But wait it is not the end.
Coming one more tedious task to bear,
Slope and deflection are coming with a fear.
Taking the beams too deep and too steep,
Without any ease and any sleep.
One method is just not enough,
Double integration is making it tough.
Macaulay method is spoiling the mood,
This slope and deflection is just not good.
Former the indicator of angle and the latter in length,
Just has hindred the beam's strength.

7. Examination of materials

Comes the chapter of examining the materials,
With a mood to spoil their main ideals.
Whether the material is failing or not ,
Factor of safety is tieing the knot.
From Tresca to Guest to Von Mises theory,
Or the other ductile or brittle theory.
All this chapter wants to know,
Whether the material is your friend or your foe.
Just keep on reading the limitations,
And in the last comes the diagram of their actions.

8. Spring of twist and turns

Very important a spring just like a finger ring,
Part that is a very important thing.
Sometimes closed coil or a helical,
All its theories are very complicated and technical.
Number of turns effect its stiffness,
Spring index has its own unique importance.
In automobiles becomes a leaf spring,
Spring is just an awesome thing.
Just has to play many important roles,
With a damper and mass has vibration controls.

9. Friction vs Viscosity

There exists a so high animosity,
One is friction and the other is viscosity.
One is hindering a solid other a fluid,
So much are their disturbing attitude.
Still neither collaborate nor can break the ice,
Their banter is hard to believe for the eyes.
One becomes coefficient of friction,
Other a kinematic or dynamic addiction.
They are going hand in the hand,
With a power of stopping all along the band.

10. Enigma of Pascal

Stress is in pascal pressure is in pascal,
All the way is the daunting task to tackle.
Stress is an internal,pressure is external,
The units are same at all interval.
Fluid gets distributed in all directions,
Pascal law grabs all the attentions.
Comes the Mega pascal and Giga version,
All the way we deal with the units conversion.
Everywhere and every analysis,
Comes the pascal unit with all its relatives.

11. Pressure vs volume

Pressure will increase volume will decrease,
So what their diagram depicts.
All the way the process is isothermal or adiabatic,
With some sense of heat flow and thermodynamics.
Important prooerties as they say,
They remain constant or they change.
Equal volumes becomes Avogadro law,
Equal temperatures becomes isothermal without any flaw.
Following the footprints of their diagrams,
Temperature and entropy come with their own ideas.

12. Tale of a discharge

I am a small or a large discharge,
Flowing from a pipe with a big spark.
Need an area and velocity to create,
Their product just gives me an open gate.
I follow the continuity law in pipes or turbines,
Venturi and Orifices give me nice drives.
In parallel.pipes I get maximized,
In series pipes I just get on one side.
All the way is my small tale,
Flowing and coming like a sale.

13. Cycles and processes love

It is not a man made cycle,
It is a matter of thermodynamics survival.
Process is trapped in a cycle knot,
Refrigation,petroleum cycle or a carnot.
Trapped in the net of pressure and volume,
Giving a feel of being a troublesome.
All the cycles and processes will follow a path,
With an arrow and with a value part.
The love is not hidden but open,
Returns to the same point in the circle.

14. Entropy power

Comes the entropy in the limelight,
Randomness of the system is in the sight.
All the way heat and the temperature,
Coming together to define their nature.
Pressure and volume diagram takes.a.backseat,
Temperature and entropy come on the driving seat.
Process is impossible,reversible or irreversible,
Or ice just.getting to melt in a numerical.
Such has been the impact.of this entropy,
It has become a system endoscopy.

15. Temperature the lead hero

Temperature is the lead hero of the course,
It is like a champion horse.
Starts from thermodynamics to fluid to heat transfer,
Or the conduction, convection or the radiation transfer.
Takes different roles and.different names,
All have different laws.and.different names.
From.dry bulb to dew.point temperature,
To source and.sink boring temperature.
Sometimes it becomes a superheated or saturated,
This range of temperature is so well.educated.
It is the lead hero of the course,
Like a.champion horse.

16. Steam table headache

Out has come the steam table headache,
All the tasks have increased.to calculate.
Only one pressure value is given in the data,
Others are to be shown from the steam data.
Cycles are refined like a Rankine ,
Calcuations are hard to solve and define.
Its friend mollier chart is giving the nightmares,
How will the student suffer from these fears?
All the way the way has come,
To.solve the problems with a cumbersome.

17. Bernaulli and Euler's entry

Along with the Euler equation comes the Bernaulli version,
With a simple and a former's integration.
Along the flow across the two points,
In a datum or along the joints.
Comes the head loss when not ideal,
Adds to the equation with a big ordeal.
Pressure ,kinetic and datum head are friends,
From the inlet end to the outlet end.
Euler is just a trailer of the law,
Its integration has a major role to follow.

18. Flow with a continuity

Along a pipe or along a junction,
Continuity equation is a major function.
Mass flow rate is to be maintained,
Continuous density has to be attained.
Works for an compressible one too,
Equation which is valid for it too.
Area will increase,velocity will decrease
Area will decrease,velocity will increase.
Still the inlet are outlet are the same,
Equation has its own name and fame.

19. Turbine and Pump conversation

Turbine told pump we are just the opposites,
If you are prime then I am the composite.
You are converting mechanical energy to hydraulic,
I am converting it vice versa thats my tactic.
Pump said yes that is right ,
You are busy too and I am also not down without a fight.
You become Pelton,Francis or Kaplan,
I become centrifugal or a reciprocating one.
Not easy to analyze our velocity triangles,
Every discharge has its own direction.
Specific speed decides our life,
You are I both need it to survive.
Turbine said yes also we are all together,
Will remain till the end forever.

20. Jet Swag

Jet has its own style and swag,
Coming high with a high velocity tag.
Attacks a plate moving or stationary,
Or a plated with an angle of swinging.
Either syymetrical or unsymmetrical plate,
It has its own cases and fate.
Jet propulsion is his major role,
Without any hiccups plays a big role.
Will affect the plate and its direction,
Neither shows any sympathy nor shows any affection.

21. Isentropic and adiabatic

The process is isentropic and adiabatic,
Process is moving ahead in a thermodynamic.
Pressure is increasing with a temperature,
Graph is following a curvature.
Ratio of specific heats is in the game,
Gaama with a value is his name.
Heat and entropy is constant,
This process has its own talent.
Take the nozzle, a diffuser or a fuel cycle,
It will come to play its part time survival.

22. Nozzle and diffuser banter

Nozzle is just a velocity booster,
Pressure just falls from a rollercoaster.
Just is compressed the big area,
Velocity is increased in the sectional area.
All the law that it makes and follows,
Diffuser comes with another plan to halt.
Increases the pressure ,decreases the velocity,
Such is their banter and animosity.
No matter how much is any type of viscosity,
But still they fight for their name and authority.

23. Chase with equation of Laplace

The chase has begun the testing has started,
Whether the equation is following Laplace needs to be sorted.
Has to check the type of flow,
Rotational flow or an irrotational flow.
Not need a single but a double deriavative,
Not found is any other alternative.
Checking the sum equal or not equal to zero,
Will make the flow existing or a non existing hero.
The chase ends of the Laplace,
In Engineering maths is just a steeplechase.

24. Matrices tricks

So many rules and so many tricks,
Matrix has so many hard tricks.
A determinant or cofactor was not enough,
Rank of it and transpose rule made it more tough.
Came the eigen value and eigen vectors,
With a hard equation of cofactors.
Inverse became tedious to calculate,
Consistency of equation needs to evaluate.
Sometimes in the analysis of stress,
Components that are giving a stress.
This matrix is playing so many tricks,
With so many logics and so many logics.

25. Iterating again

We are calculating again and iterating again,
A very complex accuracy and precise game.
One value is carrying the baton to the next,
The new one is somewhat better or best.
Many theories or many numerical methods,
All the just doing some wonder.
Someday is Newton Raphson someday is falsi method,
Someday is Euler method someday is RK method.
We need a result up to certain decimal places,
Iteration is done on a regular basis.

26. Divergence vs Curl

Neither any transpose nor any cofactors,
It is a game of Cartesian vectors.
Comes the operator called dell,
Has a new theory and concept to tell.
Dot product with the vector yields divergence,
Curl just comes with a cross product convergence.
All the way giving a sense of rotation,
Or a simple value with a notation.
Hard to understand these type of theories,
They always come like a big masterpiece.

27. Simplex so complex

Linear programming was not so linear,
Always playing its own tricks not so clear.
Out has came a new method called simplex,
Name is just only simple but is complex.
Constraints are increasing in the problem,
Slack variables are to be added soon.
Maximizing or minimizing is the goal,
Every calculation needs a careful control.
Till the end keep on solving,
Until an optimal solution starts talking.
Sometimes comes as a unbounded solution,
Mind just want it as an illusion.

28. So critical path

So critical is the path of project,
This is a somehow an interesting subject.
Critical path needs to be evaluated,
Activity and events needs to be solved and calculated.
Sometimes will become a PERT sometimes a CPM,
We need the standard deviation and variance.
Expected time is the main lead,
Other three times give it a feed.
Critical path will come as the longest,
Duration of the project will be the srtongest.

29. Toughness swag

So much is the swag so much is the toughness,
Coming from the curve of strain and stress.
The ability is to sustain impact loads,
The material seems to be very strong.
So impact and so tough is needed,
Materials like Tungsten is indeed.
The property that is a mechanical,
Always helps to find out a analysis and numerical.

30. Cast iron and steel chat.

Cast iron said I am weak and brittle,
Steel what makes you to laugh and giggle?
Steel said well I am mild and ductile,
That is low my carbon percentile.
Not more than two percent of carbon,
You are more than that two percent of carbon.
Cast iron said yes still I am grey in a lathe bed,
Always ready to take all the operation tests.
You are plain ,low or high steel,
Only your ductility makes for a credit steel.
Still we assist and help the carbon,
Not only for one purpose but a multipurpose.

31. Iron carbon diagram shades

Pure iron is just a ferrite,
Body centered becomes an austenite,
Face centered becomes a delta iron,
All the structures have their own percentage of carbon.
Various temperature will come and go,
Sometimes will becomes hypereuteciod or hypo.
Iron carbide will become.a cementite,
Six point six seven will be the percentile.
Soon ferrite and cementite will form pearlite,
Microstructures that are hard to identify.
Various temperatures and various shades,
This diagram is giving us the aspects of iron in different trades.

32. Treatment of Materials

Materials want to look good and clear,
Without ant tension and without any fear.
Comes the treatment as heat therapy,
With an aim to improve the mechanical and other property.
Sometimes becomes.a.process.of.tempering,
Further becomes martempering or austempering.
Cooling rates.are.rapid.or slow,
Different materials.will come.with a blow.
Will come the annealing and normalizing,
Furnace or air as.a.medium or.carburizing.
All will refine or upgrade the material,
Temperature and medium will become theoretical.
Structures will become hard or brittle,
Knowledge will increase more or little.

33. Creeping with time

Materials are crumbling and deteriorating with time,
Creep has come to haunt them in their prime.
Not is a sudden load but of a long time,
Many years if duration will come in the prime.
Changing the behavior from elastic to plastic,
Sometimes simple or a visco elastic.
So much impactful is this creep,
How to increase the life and how to keep.
Has become a long time dependent,
Very rude and very independent.

34. Safety factor a saviour

Out has come a factor of safety,
Design needs to face a harsh reality.
Either a design stress or a working stress,
Factor will come always to depress.
From the analysis of Soderberg of Goodman,
Or the theories of failure full of a can.
Will save or safeguard the material,
Any specimen in a design criteria.
Else the materials breaks or fails,
Nobody comes to praise it and hail.
Has done a lot of selfless favour,
Factor of safety is a saviour.

35. Elastic and plastic

Stretching a small or large rubber band,
Just with a slight force in hand.
Does not give up comes just back,
Has a sense of an elastic jack.
Regains and maintains its position,
Neither any achievement nor any mission.
Further stretched will not be the same,
Plastic behaviour will be the name.
Will not come as back as a regain,
Will lose its shape will a deformation shame.

36. Flywheel and governer chat

Flywheel asked Governor how are we different,
Governer replied I tell you an incident,
You will just store the energy for the engine,
I regulate the mean of the engine.
You are important to your coefficient of flucuation,
I am sometimes sensitive ,isochronous or non isochronous.
So many sleeve and mass to handle,
You only just take the fluctuations scandal.
Flywheel said yes we both are equally important,
Safeguarding the engine is our talent.
Only we need the support of each other.
I am your younger brother you are my elder brother.

37. Petrol and Diesel cycle conversation.

Petrol said I am sometimes gasoline,
Otto is my other name in the scene.
Working on a constant volume process,
Has less compression with a distress.
Diesel said you are a less compressed one,
I am a diesel with heavy compression one.
Working on the constant pressure,
I have much more leisure.
Although we both handle two and four stroke,
Our comparisons take on us a poke.
Sometimes efficiency or sometimes a cost,
Makes us to get somewhere lost.
Petroleum said yes our cycle is somewhat different,
We can't go in each other zone as we have different talent.

38. Dual cycle move

Very clever is this cycle of dual,
Has both petrol and cycle as a mutual.
Will take the compression or cut off ratio,
Long and complex like a tough ratio.
Always comes as an intermediate medium,
Either petrol or diesel are in the maximum.
Such a move that it plays,
Will rely on both as he says.
Such is his enigma and swag,
A dual cycle is its name and tag.

39. Damper does a hamper

Comes the mass and spring with a damper,
Vibration is stopped just a sense of hamper.
These three making a network system,
Of a free,forced or damped vibration.
Sometimes underdamped,critical or underdamped,
Logarithmically is decreasing the motion trend.
The factor that is reducing vibration,
Has long scope and many application.
Sometimes fitting in equation of motion,
Or sometimes.with a viscous tag of notion.

40. Tyre and wheel conversation

Once a tyre asked a wheel,
You are covered by me how do you feel?
Wheel replied I feel safe and secure,
You are always ready to take care.
Tyre says daily I walk on the dirt and road,
All I have to bear is a vehicle load.
Sometimes I am underflated or overinflated,
Sometimes I am burst or punctured.
Wheel said in that case I am lucky,
My design and material is always tricky.
All like me in the form of alloy,
For the youth my appearnace is like an expensive toy.
Still thankful to you as lying under your tread,
Gives me a sense of brotherhood thread.

41. Break with a brake

Vehicle said just give me a break,
I am tired and want an interval with brake.
Tyres are weared and are loosing pressure,
Brakes are giving them a time of leisure.
Either the front or the rear wheels,
All heed or obey the brake feels.
Rear obeys the handbrake in general,
Front obey the internal brake interval.
Assisting the clutch on the way,
All just wish it works long and does not fail.

42. Touch of clutch

Such a gentle or a forceful touch,
All the way is to handle a clutch.
Foot is on the clutch plate,
Driving just needs a good mate.
Controlling in the traffic or in the single way,
Clutch just comes a long way.
Types will be single or a.multiple plate,
Touch always remains a game.
Old vehicles with a large effort,
New ones with just a slight effort.
Engaging from the neutral to a gear,
Clutch has to solve all without a fear.

43. Changing the gear

Changed is the motion with a gear,
First one is shifted to the next sphere.
Gearbox is shifting its momentum,
Driving conditions are giving an ultimatum.
Form sliding mesh to constant mesh,
All the gears are coming fresh.
Spur, helical or a bevel gear,
All are important for a study sphere.
Clutch is assisting it with a tradition,
From neutral to minimum or reverse or maximum.

44. An engine' words

I am a working engine,
Coming with a spark or compression ignition.
Sometimes as a diesel or a petrol,
With a lot of hydrocarbons in its soul.
Piston is giving me a kick of stroke,
Connecting rod assists without any other scope.
I will become two or a four stroke name,
Heavy or light vehicle will recognize my name.
All I want is a fuel to run,
Power will come in a transmission system.
I am an important part of an automobile,
Battery gives me a license to start in a while.

45. Understeered and Oversteered

The wheels are slipped either front or rear,
Cause a slip with a wear and tear.
Vehicle is slipping at the front more,
Understeered is the vehicle main score.
Sharp is not a turn,its not a fun.
Slipped on the rear side more,
Oversteered has a tale to show.
Sharp is the turn ,more is the fun,
Racing cars mandates it for fun.
Getting a shake with a sharp jerk,
Steering adjustments are a must.

46. Vernier vs micrometer

Forget the name and their fame,
Vernier and micrometer are their name.
Just don't bother about their cost,
Just need their accuracy or least count.
Measuring the diameter or a small thickness,
Such is their long lasting patience.
Some manual or a digital form,
Measurement is the major norm.
These jaws or anvil or a thimble,
Have a lot to answer with a piece of single.

47. Heat and work conversation

Heat told work we both are path functions,
State is not our junctions.
Included in the first law or thermodynamics,
Sometimes we are zero in some statistics.
Work said yes I am zero or negative,
Path of yours decide my route destiny.
I add to the energy to give you,
Sometimes energy zero,I become.you.
We can't leave our same units,
Always present in every analysis.
Heat said lets keep the momentum going,
You have a good going,I too have a good going.

48. Conducting vs Radiating

Heat is flowing from one source to other,
Conduction defines it by a law of fourier.
Too long equation for solids in isotropic,
Thermal diffusivity has its own trick.
Solid to solid is the main script,
Plane wall or a cylinder depict their script.
Radiating is just with a medium,
Like the rays of a bright sun.
Emmision of some strong rays,
Boltzmann says just take my name.
Comes the white body or a black body,
Will come too emmisivity with a heavy gravity.
Can't compare the both modes,
Both have their unique properties and codes.

49. An electrode tale

I am an electode just like a stick,
Coated is a flux on my skin.
Just produces a spark where to weld,
Make sure I am just properly held.
Sometimes I consumes or no consumes,
Something all does not assume.
Take the different names like an arc,
Just will come a harmful eye spark.
Just keep me fixed and keep me tight,
Else face the problem when out of sight.

50. Laminar and turbulent conversation

Laminar asked turbulent what's is your Reynolds number,
Turbulent replied more than four thousand.
Laminar said I just sway below two thousand,
Many fluid flows are in my hand.
Sometimes steady or incompressible equation,
Give me a sense of satisfaction.
Turbulent said in that case I am unlucky,
My whole path profile is a tricky.
So much layer with a coefficient of roughness,
Always follow a motion of zigzag.
In your transition you may have experienced,
How your smooth flow faces a hinderenace.
Laminar said yes but still we have a theory,
Will always try to solve the student's curiousity and query.

Printed by Libri Plureos GmbH in Hamburg,
Germany